The Gift of Feminine Energy for You and Him

H K Queen

The Gift of Feminine Energy for You and Him

H K Queen

The Gift of Feminine Energy for You and Him Copyright © by H K Queen. All Rights Reserved.

Contents

PART I. INTRODUCTION

1. The beauty of trust

2. Your beauty

3. Polarity in relationships

4. Heal your triggers and heal in relationships

5. How men are wired

6. Receiving is powerful

7. Pleasure

8. Neediness in relationships

9. Awakening your feminine energy

10. The balance of feminine and masculine energy

- 11. When he takes his space
- 12. Let things build naturally without trying to control the outcome
- 13. Building a deeper connection
- 14. Leaning back into your feminine energy
- 15. Relationship and dating issues and how to turn things around
- 16. Moving on when a relationship ends
- 17. How to stand out from the rest
- 18. How to make a relationship last
- 19. Loving yourself
- 20. Positive affirmations

About the Author

I

Introduction

H K Queen is a feminine energy, self-love, and relationship coach. She is studying and training to become a certified Ho'oponopono practitioner, which is an ancient Hawaiian sacred practice for cleansing, healing negative emotions, guilt, shame, conflicts, forgiveness, making things right in your relationship with yourself and others. If your relationship with yourself is struggling, most likely you're struggling in your relationships with others as well. If you want to heal your relationship with others, you must first heal yourself from within. She has a passion for helping and coaching women on how to heal themselves and their relationships. She has spent years studying and learning about men, how they think, are wired, about feminine energy, and applying it to her own relationship. She has a passion for sharing her knowledge with other women about what works well with men.

1

The beauty of trust

THE GREATEST COMPLIMENT YOU CAN GIVE A MAN IS "I TRUST YOU." YOU CAN DO THIS BY SAYING THESE WORDS OR BY SHOWING IT THROUGH YOUR ENERGY. WHEN YOU LEAN BACK AND ALLOW HIM TO PURSUE YOU, YOU ARE SHOWING HIM YOU TRUST HIM.

The truth is, when you cannot trust a man to remain faithful to you or to lead the relationship, you damage the relationship. You cannot be in a healthy relationship if you do not trust. Trust all begins with trusting you are enough and trusting in your man. However, if you persist in these kinds of relationships, where you cannot trust, it is a strong clue that you have very little self-regard and it may be best to seek out guidance from a professional.

On a positive note, both partners can experience a trusting relationship. They are both at the same starting point and this is a beautiful place to be.

With the realization that the blossoming of trust between two lovers is one of the most profound experiences of human existence, it is also a brilliant foundation for a relationship to be built upon which can then soar.

First, we can all agree that both men and women each have their individual strengths and weaknesses. Keeping a realistic outlook on this very nature of humankind, we can also agree that ups and downs are a part of all relationships. When we struggle to believe in each other, we question our partner's loyalty and we question ourselves. This may not be a permanent situation, but through experience and helping my clients, I believe the truth is that you can't fully trust another until you have mastered trusting yourself.

When we suffer in our relationships, such as losing faith in our partner's loyalty, it is really a wake-up call from the universe asking you to find the lesson in your circumstances and to gain wisdom as a result. Life is constantly evolving and the good news is the positive aspects of your relationship can move forward and the negative ones will need to be resolved and forgiven.

I am a great believer in second chances. Life is school and we all learn from mistakes we have made in one area or another. Individually, we can take responsibility for our mistakes, learn from them and correct them.

Sometimes the breakdown of a relationship is not his fault. Maybe you've been domineering and operating from your masculine energy. This could cause him to look elsewhere, for a softer woman, one that will encourage him to take a more dominant role. Or maybe you frightened him away by being in a constant state of neediness. Men are more attracted to women who are self-fulfilled because they emanate joy instead of weakness and crisis mode.

Statistics show that almost every relationship will have concerns over trust at least once during their lifespan, and over half of relationships have ongoing trust issues all the time. I firmly believe that trust is the life blood of a loving relationship. With it, your passion comes alive and romance swirls about. You never take each other for granted because together you have discovered the holy grail of infinite, divine love for one another.

As human beings, we desire trust in our lives. It is a fundamental aspect of our intellect. As a species, it has allowed us to move forward in many realms. The businesses of Microsoft, Apple and Google were founded by men whose bonding required trust, especially at the onset of highly confidential, inventive technologies.

Lastly, I want to share with you the science behind trust. Biologically trust is built into humankind's DNA. We all carry the hormone of oxytocin, which can be released by both men and women. This is a bonding, feel-good hormone which, when emitted, is optimal for human health both psychologically and physically. After a long embrace, when these hormones are released, people experience great joy and feelings of panic and anxiety leave the system. In our relationships, this can be helpful as it acts as a glue between partners who share the euphoria feeling that oxytocin supplies them. It is this biological fusion that will help relationships endure and stand the test of time.

Trust is a beautiful feeling. Start now by trusting in your worth and value. Trust the man or men in your life and allow the Universe to guide you on a beautiful journey of love.

Your beauty

The journey towards a woman's inner and outer beauty is a lifelong pursuit.

We all start at some point. You may have suffered a terrible loss or a painful break-up of a relationship with someone you deeply loved. Maybe you have suffered for years because you were never told you were beautiful as you grew up. Whatever the case is, you must begin your journey by letting go of the past hurt, having faith in who you are, and be fully in the present. All possibilities are found in the present. All the losses you may have felt in the past because you believed you weren't good enough or beautiful enough should be cast aside because they are no longer relevant in each new moment you experience. They are all just stories, memories, they aren't real; you are beautiful, and you are enough.

First of all, I would like to say that you have an important responsibility to your friends, to yourself, male counterparts and family to be the most beautiful incarnation of yourself, particularly when it comes to inner beauty. Twisting and manipulating relationships and the stories you used to bolster such poor behavior will negate all beauty because it will show up as a lack of a moral compass in everything you do or say.

A pure, honest life instead of one of deceit and lies will go a long way. People will feel these genuine characteristics emanating from you and will seek you out for reasons being mainly the properties of the goodness you exude.

One of your secret powers, when you are aligned with truth, is that you are in touch with your divine, higher self. This is the source of the greatest light you can bring forth into the world. You will shine very brightly in the world because of this inclination. You will be acting from a higher source and your zest for life and energy will soar.

The negative influences in your life will be repelled as your spirit becomes uplifted. You will attract better people who understand the significance of your goodness and may even be on a similar path. You will also renounce all burdens that are not truly yours as you grow lighter and lighter. People will feel blessed in your presence.

Renew your mind daily with breathing technique exercises or meditation. Peace and quiet first thing in the morning for an hour or two, while sipping tea or lemon water, it will cleanse both the system and the mind before plugging into your electronic devices. Journaling is also a good early morning practice. Doing this at the start of each day will bring clarity to your mind. It will also help you move through your day more aware of seeing how many gifts you really do have just by being a person alive on this earth.

In self-care, you walk away from negative behaviors such as negative self talk, neglecting yourself, seeking approval from others, judgement toward yourself and others, because your divine self repels such activities.

Many women don't know that they are born free. She should know that her freedom and pursuit of happiness are not selfish acts, but rather necessary in creating a beautiful life. Radiating this message to others is a great deed and in turn will release others from the feelings of living a shackled life. Thus beauty is not just how you look, but what you do in your life to better humanity.

Poet John Keats, in the 19th century, put it well in his poetry when he wrote, "Beauty is truth, truth beauty." By removing impure thoughts and activities, we actually have a rebirth of the soul which is not tethered to earthly desires. Shedding this aspect of our nature helps to rebuild confidence in ourselves other than material happiness which comes and goes with only momentary joy. We become aligned with the best version of ourselves, leaving behind all things that don't serve us well.

As a woman, your gifts of creativity, concern for the well-being of others, humility and divine light all add up to a fertile, exponentially growing beauty where you will be seen in such a light. You will also be heard.

Speak kindly of others and yourself. Do not let anyone tell you how you should live your life. By now you have already reached deep within to find your purpose and wisdom. You have no reason to feel intimidated by others or insecure about your place on earth. Simply allow your unique beauty and light to burst forth!

Be comfortable in your own skin. Remember not to compare yourself with other women.

As an enlightened human being, you realize everyone is unique with their own particular gifts and their own interpretations of beauty. Do away with self-doubt and negative thinking. Don't be afraid to reach beyond your comfort zone. A friend once said to me, "Reach for the stars and you'll end up with the moon."

Secretly, in silence, your calling will be whispered to you in the wind. Pay attention to these divine messages as they may come unexpectedly at any time. Always allow room for these divine downloads. They will surely arrive as long as you keep space for them and have faith in the universe's intelligence.

As you find time for self-care, you will cleanse your body, soul and home. When you do this, you get rid of both physical debris and psychological debris. With such a cleanse, we become more attractive to both men and women. Our victories grow in number as we glow in the light of the divine. Our courage will also intensify as we own ourselves and take full responsibility for all that happens as a result of our actions.

With the knowledge that there is a divine plan for everyone, you will feel confident in fulfilling your divine destiny. Instability will no longer have a hold over you. This balance will become apparent in both your mind and the peacefulness you exude. Balance is beauty.

A sight to see. You have become!!!

3

Polarity in relationships

In any healthy, successful, and long lasting relationship there has to be polarity. Polarity in human relationships creates the spark that occurs between two opposites, masculine and feminine energies. Even same-sex relationships need a healthy balance between masculine and feminine energies, or the relationship will not last.

We all have masculine and feminine energy, but there are women who are more masculine at their core, as well as men who are more feminine at their core. The way that nature has it, most men are more masculine, and most women are more feminine. However, due to women's inner struggles and wounds, many operate out of their more aggressive masculine energy. Also, due to the feminist movement, women have freedom to compete with men in the jobs arena. A lot of women are successful in their business, work, or career goals, which requires that they operate out of their masculine energy.

Women need to learn how to balance their energies. It's okay to be in your masculine energy at work, or on your own when you have to get the job done. When you come home to your man, you need to learn how to leave the pants at work: rest, be still, lean back, and let the man wear the pants.

Yes, some women are more comfortable functioning more in their masculine energy, just as some men are more comfortable operating in their feminine energy. However, most women want a man who is a protector and provider, and confident in leading the relationship. Most men desire women who are soft, sweet, receptive, and willing to follow his leadership. Problems can arise when a woman is operating more in her masculine energy, and a man is operating more in his feminine energy. If two people who are dating or in a relationship have the same energies, the relationship will not last.

If two people have the same energies, then the sexual attraction and/or chemistry between them won't start, grow or last. When two people have the same energies, there will also be conflicts, resentments, and other issues that will damage the relationship.

If you're a woman who is having a hard time attracting men, keeping men, or problems arise in your relationships, be aware of your energy, because most likely you are operating out of your masculine energy. In order to have success in dating and relationships, practice functioning more in your feminine energy.

4

Heal your triggers and heal in relationships

Do your inner work and inner child healing. When you feel triggered you must go within and learn how to sit through your painful feelings without blaming yourself or anyone else every time they come up. Learn how to stop blaming others as well. Your triggers are your responsibility to sit and work through, fix and heal. It isn't anyone else's job to soothe you or make you feel good. What you've been through in life isn't all your fault, however, it's your responsibility to heal.

You have to work through your past wounds and emotional baggage so they don't affect you or your relationship. Learn how to observe your reactions to your partner, the stories you tell yourself about you and him. Nine times out of ten, you're creating your own drama from experiences. I'm not saying some men can't be toxic, but if you're constantly having toxic relationships, you are most likely attracting that into your life because of how you feel inside. When you work on your triggers, there's a strong possibility the men in your life will respond differently to you. And if they don't, you'll be ready to let go of that chapter of your journey, because it isn't serving you anymore and you'll attract better.

You can heal in a relationship. Your partner is holding a mirror up to you so you can heal those parts of yourself that need healing, and once you've healed, your relationship will too, unless other issues prevent it from doing so. If that is the case, someone else better will soon come along.

When something uncomfortable comes up in your relationship and you feel triggered, pause, take a step back, breathe, and try to see things from different perspectives. Is your partner doing things to upset you, treating you badly, or are you telling yourself stories that aren't true? Look at things from his standpoint. What's causing your partner to act the way he does, is he responding to your reactive, masculine energy, or does he have healing to do as well?

Take a time out, take space, or breathe. Feel your feelings without judgments and being in your head. What do you feel? Do you feel sad, angry, irritated, scared or mad? Write it out in a journal. It's okay. Learn to self-soothe and let the feelings pass, because they will. Know that everything will be okay.

Do you feel insecure? Do you suffer from childhood abandonment issues? Learn to love yourself and let your inner child know she's loved. Realize your value. When you feel insecure, you are too focused on something you feel is lacking in yourself. To feel more secure in a relationship, it helps to know what you have to offer to the other person. You don't have to be a supermodel or have a perfect body. Energy is more important, and so is character. Looks get women in the door, but it's feminine energy that makes her a keeper.

Build your self-esteem. When you aren't feeling good about who you are on the inside, it is natural to want to look outside of yourself for validation. You don't need validation from anyone. You are enough. Stop comparing yourself to other women. Instead, compliment them. Realize that you are beautiful and unique. There's no one like you, and that is your power.

Trust in yourself. Feeling secure in a relationship not only depends on trusting the other person, but on learning to trust yourself as well. Trust yourself to know that no matter what the other person does, you will take care of you. Trust yourself that you are enough. Trust him to lead you to the right place. Trust that your higher power will hold you every step of the way.

Practice self compassion. Speak nicely and positively to yourself. Nurture yourself and do good things for you so that you can feel good and be happy.

Stop entertaining those negative thoughts. Replace negative thoughts with positive thoughts about you. Think about and reflect on the good. Remember compliments people say to you. Write out good things about yourself when you're feeling insecure. Take a few minutes each day to list ten things you appreciate about yourself. Practice positive affirmations. Replace I am not, with I am. I am enough; I am beautiful; I am loved; I am a goddess. You can add others as well.

Practice meditation. Even if it's for five minutes a day. Listen to meditations on letting go of hurt, self-esteem, insecurities and more.

At the end of the day, you have all the power to heal yourself and your relationships with men. It all comes down to loving yourself more, letting go of past hurt and memories, doing your inner work and rewriting your story.

5

How men are wired

Emotional triggers are things that make you feel psychological pain. Can cause you to react in uncontrollable ways. They all come from past injuries, such as painful memories of negative situations, and childhood traumas. When you feel triggered your emotions can cause reactions that result in tantrums, anxiety, depression, fear, and panic. If you don't learn how to heal or deal with your triggers, they'll control you, damage you and harm your relationships with others, especially men. Men do not want to be with a woman who is always upset and bothered by everything.

Learn how to take accountability for actions. Take ownership of your life. We often underestimate how much control we have over our destinies.

We attract what we are; we attract our own mess. If you continue attracting men who are toxic, work on healing and work on changing your energy. You take emotional ownership of your feelings and work through them on your own. Know you are enough, you are divine, you are loved, you deserve love and that your higher power wants you to be free of your emotional wounds and happy.

Learn how to self-soothe yourself and your own emotions. Those are your responsibility. Meditate, forgive yourself and forgive others. Talk positively to yourself; show compassion, love, and kindness to yourself and others.

Men are born and wired to be natural leaders and hunters. They go after what they want in their careers, workplace, and with women.

Because of how they are wired, men seek out sex, but they want relationships just as much as women do. Sex doesn't prevent a man from going deeper with you. It's how you act afterwards. You must always remain carefree. On the one hand, he may need to take time to get into a place where he feels worthy of having the total package of sex and love. For the woman, patience is key. Giving him drama-free space to put it all together is required. Be calm and not demanding while he sorts himself out.

Most contemporary men understand the old male-female relationship paradigms are out-of-date. As people, we have all evolved so much in the last 10 years. There has been an enormous awakening in men of what is no longer acceptable behavior. Men know they must shatter their previously held perceptions, yet remain empowered and at peace with their new principles, particularly in their relationships with women. With this awakening, they will discover new concepts of power and a new understanding of women's needs, desires and the respect they long for from men.

It is the dream of men to stand fully anchored, in their own power, with energy and confidence. Women and the world at large respond well to those qualities. Men are becoming liberated at this moment, just as women have come to enjoy their freedom and keep abreast as the new paradigms shift. Men have made the commitment to evolve and embrace the new dynamics between men and women so that they can thrive in all areas of their lives. The truth is, women crave these newly evolved men; the ones who have rewired themselves to be strong, masculine, and confident and care about women and their desires.

Men who haven't evolved are losing their grip on their purpose, perform below average at work and in their family life. Many are miserable in their relationships because the energy is stale and outmoded. They are easily intimidated by other men who have modernized and women who have found freedom exhilarating and their joy in finding partners who are liberated as well.

Traditional relationships went out the door and a new phase began as women have gradually been achieving equal rights and have demonstrated to men that they weren't needed to be self-sufficient. Because of the great deal of confusion men were having as women progressed, they no longer understood what actually worked when it came to pleasing women. Men had to be shown again that women still wanted them to lead, to be strong and to make decisions both inside and outside the home. When your man does properly lead, he needs to be shown appreciation which will help reinforce his confidence and courage.

There is a fork in the road that all men face regarding their masculine leadership. The first choice is to remain in the old paradigm where he is harsh, bossy, and misogynistic when the woman is in her masculine energy. The second choice, within the new paradigm, is being a strong leader who is peaceful, protective, and cherishes his woman. The first is toxic, the second, a dream to be around for all. He is powerful but behaves with goodness in his heart. These men attract women who want them to lead because they are kind and respectful of boundaries. People work to please him out of loyalty and not fear.

Men are secretly learning that they can reinforce their leadership both at home and in the workplace without taking away women's feminine power. They are learning that being grounded in their masculinity is more attractive to women than playing "Mr. nice guy".

Women instead still want the luxury of safety that men are wired to provide. An evolved man knows how to lead and enjoys his connection with women. She positively reinforces him, and his confidence soars. Men are often mistaken to think they are losing their power in contemporary times. When they join in with the evolution, instead of fighting it, they will soon come to realize that by the mere act of holding space for a woman's divine power, they will not lose their own masculine power. It is important for men to know that their ancient wiring of tapping into their desires has not changed. It is natural. Because it will always be there, perhaps now they will fulfill their desires in a more thoughtful, sensitive way.

No male or female partner should endure constant criticism, toxicity in the home or being with a controlling, insensitive bullying partner. Both men and women have been guilty of these traits.

The new wiring for men is happening at such a rapid pace. Men are reinventing masculine power in such a pleasurable way, that enlightened women are finding these evolved men as being more seductive than ever. These men know both how to lead and love women at the same time, which completes the circle of men's new wiring.

Let it be, and so it is.

6

Receiving is powerful

Receiving is feminine energy. Feminine energy is knowing you are worth it to receive. You receive all the good things in life from The Universe and your man. This is what allows us to feel pleasure.

You are responsible for being in your divine feminine energy. Allowing yourself to be still, responding to and expressing how you feel moment to moment (positive feelings) all in appropriate ways.

Yin energy is feminine energy, which is receiving energy. Yang energy is masculine energy, which is giving and doing. Your power as a feminine woman is to receive.

When you can receive from a man, you will feel wonderful inside and so will he. A man wants to provide for you and make you happy. Allow the men or man in your life to step up and invest in the relationship by giving to you, taking you out, pursuing you, and helping you. When you can receive all that a man has to offer by being receptive, grateful and appreciative, your relationship with him will deepen. When we cannot receive from a man, it makes him think as though he is not needed in your life and he will eventually go searching for a woman who operates more in her feminine energy and knows how to receive.

Learn how to receive without feeling guilty or that you owe something in return. Just accept the good things he has to offer and show genuine gratitude.

7

Pleasure

Instead of the angrily desired feminist freedom, women can secretly have all the freedom she desires by being in her feminine energy. By taking care of and loving herself. She does this by rooting herself in her wholeness and connecting to the infinite divine universe, something much larger than herself. In this place, she doesn't need to repress anything and because of this her self-love can soar! This type of freedom that she connects to is her greatest light, and the beauty of it all is that men desire women in this state more than anything. Not needing anyone to make her feel complete or whole.

Her vibes of inner freedom actually excite him in the most powerful way! She's independent, yet, she'll allow a man to step up, help her, and do for her without force or pressure. To get to this freedom, a woman must take care of herself by making her own pleasure her priority. Remember, you come first. Always nurture yourself.

Find pleasure in every day. Receive sexual pleasure. Buy flowers for yourself, play your favorite music and dance. Do things that bring you joy. Find pleasure in everything you do. Read, write, be creative, meditate, relax, take a bath, light a candle, sip on your favorite drink, and cook your favorite meal. Experience pleasure all around you and be open to receive it. Know that you deserve it.

8

Neediness in relationships

When a woman is constantly needy with a man or in her relationships, her man might try to make her feel better for a little while. But, eventually her neediness will become a source of pain to him and turn him off. Her low self-worth and self-esteem will begin to annoy him and he'll see her as low value. Her neediness will become too much for him. Eventually he'll go on the search for a woman that exudes self-love, confidence, and one who doesn't seek out validation from others to believe she is enough.

Neediness can and will ruin a relationship if a woman does not heal and get a handle of it.

I'm sure in the beginning of the relationship you acted carefree. While getting to know him, you were more desirable because you were more relaxed, and he was attracted to you because of that. As the relationship progressed, you started showing signs of neediness, and you started to push him away. Always keep the same energy that you have in the beginning of the relationship by caring less, keeping a life outside of him and the relationship and if he isn't a boyfriend keep dating others.

Being needy will cause a man to shut you out. If you became needy after the relationship progressed, he will have doubts about you and the relationship. In his mind, you aren't acting like the woman he fell for when you both first started dating and this will cause him to resent you. His trust in you will disappear.

To stop being needy with men, learn how to take care of your own needs and not depend on him for your happiness or validation. Recognize you have a problem with neediness and it needs to be fixed. Do your inner work and seek out guidance from a professional that can help you heal your inner wounds and help you learn how to cultivate self-love and self-esteem.

Realize you are enough and you don't need anyone's approval to know that you are.

Awakening your feminine energy

Feminine energy is mostly about receiving, being still and trusting the process of life. She is mysterious. She talks less and listens more. Feminine energy is soft and sweet. Masculine energy is doing, competitive, assertive, controlling, analytical, driven, focused, strong, and logical. Feminine energy is receptive, soft, accepting, allowing, open, cooperative, understanding, free, happy, playful, carefree, and easygoing. Feminine energy is about being instead of doing. Feminine energy is learning how to be still. Feminine energy requires you to be receptive. Be open to receive help, love, affection, support, compliments, and a man investing in you.

To awaken your feminine energy, get creative, move, dance, meditate, go out in nature, breathe, enjoy a sacred space, relax, and just be. Go with the flow of life and in your relationships with men. Feminine energy is about slowing down and relaxing, letting go and allowing the flow of life and relationships to happen naturally without any force. It's about being present in this moment and enjoying the now.

Take time out to take care of and nurture yourself because self-care and self-love is important. Love yourself, from there it is safe to be vulnerable, and have healthy boundaries that come naturally. You are protected with no need for walls. Your power to attract is phenomenal! From self-love you can notice if a man's energy is natural and respectful. If a man's actions are authentic, your self-appreciation will start to expand.

For women, being soft is your strength. Have faith and trust in it. This may be difficult at first, but it will become healing for you and your relationships with men. It inspires high value masculine men who are truly interested in you to step up, protect and invest in you. To trust in your feminine energy takes time, but with practice you'll find that it's absolutely worth it and so are you!

As women we can get into thoughts, thinking that men just want a woman with beautiful breasts, a perfect complexion. However, when asked, what they really want is a woman who is receptive, sweet, soft, open, confident and sensuous. A woman who's comfortable being in her feminine energy.

To be sensual, a woman needs to be fully in her body which gives a glow and magnetism, which is true feminine magic and very powerful. Reclaim your feminine power!

Women have an infinite source of light that we bring forth to the world and our relationships. This light we naturally process heals the world. Don't be afraid to let your light shine. Embrace your feminine energy for true liberation. It is the most natural, beautiful, and powerful part of who you are! To be in her feminine energy a woman must functioning in her masculine energy. She must become grounded and allow things to flow naturally. Embrace your feminine energy for true liberation. It is the most natural, beautiful, and powerful part of who you are!

10

The balance of feminine and masculine energy

You need a balance of feminine and masculine energy for a relationship to build and last.

You play a powerful role by being in your feminine energy. You inspire high value men who are interested in you to step into their masculine energy when you lean back into your feminine energy.

If the balance of feminine and masculine energy is off, the relationship problems will arise. When a man operates more in feminine energy, it repels a feminine woman. When a woman is functioning more in her masculine energy, it repels a masculine man. You play a powerful role by being in your feminine energy because you inspire high value men who are truly are interested in you to step into their masculine energy and pursue you.

Women should be more in their feminine energy, and men should be more in their masculine energy. Embrace your feminine energy. Your feminine energy is powerful, heals, and inspires those around you, especially men.

If the balance of feminine and masculine energy is off, the relationship will have problems. When a man is more in his feminine energy, it repels a feminine woman. When a woman is more in her masculine energy, it repels a masculine man. That's why it is important to learn how to be in your feminine energy. A masculine man craves his opposite, a woman who knows how to be in her feminine energy. Feminine energy is powerful. When you step into your feminine energy you create a healthy balance in your relationships and you allow a very strong bond, attraction and connection to build.

We all possess both energies. However, it's meant for most men to operate more in their masculine energy, and most women to shine more in their feminine energy. It's important to learn how to balance both energies. Learn how to use your masculine energy in your career and work area if you have to, but with men and in your relationship, throw it away, drop your pants and put on your skirt, allow him to wear the pants and trust him to do so.

When you can allow the flow of masculine and feminine energy, you and your relationship will experience a shift that is so powerful and healing. You'll appreciate your man more, and he'll appreciate you as well. From that point your relationship will continue to blossom and stand strong.

11

When he takes his space

When a man takes space, let him be. Let him pull away! Don't chase him or try to close in the gap. If you allow him to pull back without worrying or chasing, you allow him the opportunity to come back, ready to shower you with more affection.

When men are so busy doing and putting energy into us and our relationship, they need a break and time to rest and recharge. Let them get their alone time, let them take a break and bounce back after recharging. When he pulls away keep the focus on you. This is the perfect time to enjoy your own life, make yourself happy, nurture yourself, hang out with friends and lean back into your feminine energy.

When he comes toward you again, because most likely he will, just be soft, sweet, open and receptive. Don't accuse him, blame him, make him feel bad, act mean, or interrogate him by asking questions of where he's been. Act like you didn't notice the space. Be happy to hear from him as though nothing happened because you are too busy living your fabulous life. If it's a man you're dating, you are too busy dating other men to worry about his absence. If it's a man you are just dating, see others so you won't be focusing only on him when he pulls back. If he's a boyfriend, spend time with family and friends, fill yourself up.

Don't be afraid of space. Remember, men fall for you with space and their feelings grow deeper when they have time to miss you and about the beautiful memories you both shared. Next time the man you're in a relationship with or dating takes space, let him be, they'll most likely bounce back, eventually. Be okay on your own, no matter the outcome.

12

Let things build naturally without trying to control the outcome

Having a healthy relationship with a man requires you to step fully into your feminine energy. It's about trusting yourself, him, and the process. It's about not jumping ahead of a man with fantasies about the future and over-investing. If you are single, you must enjoy dating multiple men at one time until claimed without being desperate for a certain outcome. Drop your expectations and have fun in dating and relationships. Have patience and allow things to flow naturally. Remember, anything worth having, like a great relationship, takes time and needs to build first. Don't be in a rush and hurry to settle down, and please, never settle. Always choose the man who's stepping up and choosing you consistently. A man's actions will show how he truly feels about you and how much time and energy he's investing into you and the relationship.

When you meet a man, let him pursue you and ask for your number, do not go up to him and give him your number, if he's interested he'll ask for yours. If you are on a dating site and a man leaves you his number, you can simply reply back with yours if you are interested. Now the ball is in his court, you can sit back, relax and observe if he's truly interested. If he is, he'll make a move.

Don't initiate contact by calling, texting, and Facebook messaging just to check to what he is doing. Don't stay in his face to remind him you exist, he already knows. He knows where and how to connect with you. When the relationship progresses and you both are committed to each other, you can initiate sometimes, if you feel comfortable, but observe how your man acts afterwards and don't constantly do it. However, a masculine man who's interested in you will not mind courting you no matter how long you've both been together as long as you appreciate him and his efforts. But I would strongly advise you to allow him to pursue you throughout the whole process.

Don't give up your life, friends or other men when first dating a man. Don't put all your eggs in one basket with him, especially in the beginning. Don't wait around for him to make plans with you, go out and live. Don't offer advice when he talks about his life and work. I know you think you're being helpful, but you're leading and trying to fix with your masculine energy. Just listen and keep your mouth closed. In our minds, we think we're being caring, thoughtful and sweet. The truth is, it's a form of mothering and a turn off.

If we want a man in our life who knows what he wants, we should allow him the space to step up because he knows what he wants and that's us. We don't do the work for him. We give him both the space and the opportunity to pursue us. When we take a step back and give men space, pay attention to his actions, it'll show us how much effort and time he's putting in with us. That way we don't chase him away or waste our time on a man who isn't really interested.

If things don't match between you and a man, don't give up, keep being open to other men and keep living your life. Don't take rejection or him not being ready for anything personal. Wish him well and know that there are plenty of other fish in the sea. Not everyone is a match and not everyone is ready for a commitment. Respect it and don't try to change or go against his decision.

Never get ahead of a man by obsessing, pining or plotting. This will save you from heartache and being heartbroken.

Building a deeper connection

If you want to build a connection with a man, you must first learn how to be more feminine and lean back. Learn how to relax and enjoy the moment with him without jumping ahead. Men are naturally drawn to women who are able to be fully present in the moment. They are less attracted to women who are constantly wondering about the future. Never jump ahead of him with commitment. It will only push him away and damage any potential you have for the relationship going deeper. Always be on the same page and allow him to pursue you. If you can learn how to let him process his feelings and move the relationship forward while you relax in your inviting feminine energy, he'll be inspired to come closer and build a stronger bond with you. Your feminine energy inspires a man to fall in love with you. When he knows he makes a difference in your world, it's easy for him to become emotionally connected and invested in you. When glowing in your feminine energy he will be inspired to step up, provide for you, protect you, do things that would make you happy, lead the relationship, and build an emotional bond with you. This is what creates polarity and an emotional connection. Always show gratitude and appreciation when he steps up for you.

You never want him to do anything because you told him to or try to force him. If you try to control or force him, it'll turn him off and he won't build a connection with you. Trust him by first trusting yourself that you are worthy of love and a man who loves you.

Don't depend on your partner to fill you up. Have a life outside of him and your relationship. Fill up your own cup. Take care of you. You come first. Don't react to everything he does or doesn't do. When you react, you create problems in the relationship, you push him away and damage the polarity in the process. Each time you react to something you're damaging any chance of him connecting with you because now he will not feel safe. He will not think it is safe to come closer to you or show his emotions. Learn to relax and breathe.

So, relax, chill out and have fun!

14

Leaning back into your feminine energy

What is leaning back into your feminine energy about? It's about putting and keeping the focus on you. It's about not trying to control what a man does or doesn't do, how the relationship should go or trying to control the outcome. It's about believing in your worth and knowing you are worth a man pursuing you.

Always have a sense of mystique in the beginning and throughout the relationship with any man. Keep them wondering. Save your personal information. He doesn't need to know everything about you or whatever you're doing, have done, or who you've slept with. He doesn't need to know about all the negative things you've been through in the past. Do not text or call a man first, especially in the beginning. This is considered pursuing and you will over invest in him when you pursue him so allow him to be the one to reach out to you. Let him lead, you follow and always be on the same page as him. Don't jump ahead ever in any stage of the courting process or relationship.

Never pursue or chase a man. When you chase anything that is a strong an indication that they are running away from you. Chasing or pursing a man will never work unless you want a guy who operates more in his feminine energy and you will eventually lose attraction for him in the process, you will resent him, and the polarity will be off.

Leaning back is about not being in your head constantly worrying or analyzing a man's every move. Stay in the present moment and stop creating fantasies about him or your relationship in your head. Lean back energetically by keeping the focus on you. When he isn't around, he shouldn't fill your mind.

Have no agenda with any man. Don't try to make anything happen with him. It is when you don't think of ways to make him love you more, push for your relationship to move forward, or worry about what you need to do to keep him interested. You actually don't have to do anything to keep him interested. Just be your fabulous self and get rid of any baggage if need be.

When you're in leaning back energy and your man leans forward, just be open, soft, receptive and respond to him. When you respond with happiness and gratitude, you show your interest in him, and this will show him with your actions that when he pursues you he is winning.

Leaning back allows you to see if a man is truly interested in you or how much effort he's putting in. Leaning back prevents you from jumping ahead of a man, pushing or scaring him away. Leaning back prevents you from investing so much into a man. Leaning back prevents you from being desperate, needy, anxious or acting out in crazy ways.

Leaning back allows a man to develop feelings for a woman he already has an attraction for. It helps him develop an emotional connection to you, fall for you and invest in you and the relationship.

Leaning back keeps his attraction and desire growing stronger towards you.

Leaning back is about being still and trusting the process. When you lean back, you give up control over a man and how the relationship develops. You give up control of the outcome. You give your man or the men you're dating space. You take your energy off of them and place it on you, taking good care of and loving you. You allow space between you and the men in your life so he can think about you and can feel the desire to come back to you and move the relationship forward. Leaning back inspires a man who's interested in you to cherish you and make you his woman.

You just have to enjoy the moment with him without jumping ahead of him. Leaning back will help you be on the same page as a man always, so you won't be left with a broken heart.

15

Relationship and dating issues and how to turn things around

Are you having issues in your relationships or dating? Do you react to everything a man does or doesn't do? If so, you need to learn to control your emotions. If you're too emotional, it is too much for a man to handle and too much drama. If you can't control your emotions, it's time to go within, work on your triggers, heal and stop making others responsible for the way you act and think. You are more powerful than you think. You can't control what others do or say outside of you. However, you can learn how to control yourself and your emotions by not giving your power away to any man.

Do you constantly criticize your partner or the men you are dating? If you do, then you need to stop because you are damaging the relationship.

Do you constantly compete with your man or the men you date? Competing is a form of masculine energy. When you compete with a man by trying to prove how intelligent you are, not being able to receive from him, you are making him feel like less of a man and you are damaging your relationship with him in the process.

Do you act clingy in your relationships? You must allow your man or the men you date space. Don't be clingy, needy, controlling, or possessive. Men love and long for freedom, even in relationships. Actually, you should love your space and freedom as well.

When in a committed relationship or marriage don't embarrass your man or try to make him look bad, in private or in front of other people. Carry yourself with dignity and grace and be a woman he will be proud to show off. Accept your man for who he is without trying to fix him or change him. If you're not happy then leave. Don't stay to make yourself or your partner miserable.

Most women are conditioned to operate in their masculine energy and try to fix problems, manage and control things in relationships. Trying to fix him or the relationship will damage things and his attraction for you. Allow things to be, instead of trying to fix. Work on you instead, and once you change your energy, you can inspire him to respond differently to you. It's a man's job to help solve and fix your relationship problems. In order to keep the polarity alive, lean back and focus on you. Whenever you and your man are having a problem in the relationship or he's pulling away, allow him to pull away. Do nothing and just be. Even when he wants or takes space you should lean back and be still. Let him bounce back to you when he is ready to fix things or ready to shower you with more love.

Never create drama, react, whine, nag, try to control him or the outcome, pressure or complain. If you must express feelings, please make sure they're positive feelings. When he does something you don't like, takes you for granted, or disrespects you in any way, you don't scream at him or be mean back, you can tell him once, but you don't need to, you let your actions speak for you; you separate yourself with distance.

Stop being controlling or trying to manipulate him. You will cause power struggles in your relationships because he will try to show you who's boss, he'll try to prove to you who's really the man in the relationship and cause him to pull away or eventually leave the relationship.

Disagreements happen. You do not have to be reactive, rude or argue to try to get your point across. Wanting to be right all the time is not worth it, especially if it damages a relationship with a man you love. Arguing is not going to get your point across. He is allowed his views on certain things and to feel the way he does. Most of the time it's best to let things slide and go.

Don't give advice to him or try to fix him or his issues for him. That would be mothering and saying to him with actions you do not believe in him or his ability as a grown man to handle his own issues. Be a good listener and don't interrupt. If he asks for advice, let him know that whatever he feels is the right thing to do, he should do it, that you know he will figure out what is best for him. All he needs is for you to be present and hear him out, he can fix things by himself. Don't pressure him to speak about your relationship problems. Don't drag him into relationship counseling. Do not tell him what to do or try to be his counselor or therapist. Give him space and allow him to be. He's a grown man, he can and will handle things on his own.

Do not make him wrong for how he chooses to handle his problems. Do not hold grudges against him. Do not have anger and resentment towards him. Practice forgiveness, acceptance and understanding. It is better to experience love and peace rather than being right all the time or damaging your relationship.

16

Moving on when a relationship ends

Ending a relationship is never easy, and it's much harder when you still love him. When relationships end usually someone wants the relationship back. I know it may sting a bit but realize a breakup isn't the end of the world, the pain won't last forever and you will find love again. Take a few days to grieve, then reconnect with yourself. Do things you stopped doing while you were in a relationship with him. Do things you love and enjoy. Reconnect with friends. If you gave up things you enjoyed doing while being with him, let this be a lesson, never give up your life for any man. Always maintain a life outside of your man and relationship.

Be open to date again. Open yourself up to other men. You probably still love your ex, but if you want to get him back or move on you must redirect your energy from him to you. Allow other men to step up in your life. Realize you'll meet other men. Be open to better and greater opportunities with men. This will help if you want to get over him or to attract him back. You will not get him back by staying stuck, depressed, sad all the time or locking yourself in the house obsessing about him. Have you ever heard when women couldn't care less or move on, their exes bounce back to them? It's because their energy is no longer on them.

Stop beating yourself up. If you made mistakes, let this be the opportunity to go within and work on those recurring issues or negative patterns. If you have inner work that needs to be done, now is the perfect time to heal so that the same toxic behaviors won't resurface again in a new relationship or with your ex if you both get back together.

Do not lose hope or faith in love. Love will happen again if you allow it to and be open to it. There will be other men you'll be attracted to and other men that will pursue you. Do not act like a victim, do not hold on to grudges, you can't move on that way and you will bring that energy into another relationship. Practice forgiveness for yourself and him, acceptance and letting go.

17

How to stand out from the rest

How do you stand out from the rest of women in the world? Be different! Be high value and never chase after any man. Practice being in your feminine energy because a man in his masculine energy can't resist a woman who's relaxed, fun, confident, and glowing with feminine energy.

How do you become high value? Never hand over your commitment too easily. A man only gets your commitment and loyalty if he steps up consistently and claims you with his actions before anything. Never chase or pursue any man. Do not obsess over any man, do not worry about where he is, who he is with or what he is doing. Never ask him where the relationship is going. Never act jealous or compare yourself to any other woman. Never compare yourself to anyone. You are enough.

Never put your life on hold to wait around for any man. Do not be loyal and shut down all of your options for a man who isn't committed to you. That is low value and not good!

Enjoy the moment when you are with him. When you both go your separate ways, enjoy your alone time without constantly thinking about him. Don't hang on to him or be afraid to lose him.

Do not be afraid to walk away if there is any abuse or constant disrespect.

Always stay in and shine in your feminine energy.

Do not go out of your way to do things for him or try to please him. Never try to take care of him as if he is helpless. Do not buy him gifts so he will pick you, it will never work because you are stepping into the masculine role. As a feminine woman you must receive. Do not give him money or try to mother him. Your job is to sit back, allow him to give and do for you and you show gratitude, appreciation and say thank you. If you want to stick out from the rest, be high value, believe in your worth and believe you are worth it to receive, because you are!

18

How to make a relationship last

Do you want to know how to make a relationship last? Stay in your feminine energy and keep the relationship polarized. How do you keep the relationship polarized? Allow him to be the man in the relationship and you be the woman. Lean back and allow him to move closer towards you in his own time. Be soft and sweet with him. Love him unconditionally for who he is right now without wanting him to be different or trying to change him.

Allow him to invest in you and compliment him sincerely when he does things for you. Show him that he is deeply appreciated for his efforts. Once you both have settled into your marriage or relationship, do not let yourself go and do not revolve your life around him. Respect, accept, understand, and listen to him and don't criticize him. Do not make him wrong in any way. Accept him for who he is. If you are not satisfied or happy, then let him go. Always give him space to be free. Enjoy your space, too. Do not hound him or nag him. Communicate without accusing or blaming him.

Enjoy the moment and do not lose who you were at the beginning of the relationship when you were fun, carefree and easygoing.

Loving yourself

A woman who loves herself is magnetic, she's irresistible. When you love yourself, you can feel safe to be vulnerable. Healthy boundaries will come naturally and not the hard boundaries that do not allow love in. You are protected with no need for walls. Your power to attract is phenomenal!

From self-love you can feel if a man's energy is natural and respectful. If a man's actions are authentic, your self-appreciation will start to expand. He will feel good too when you can receive him because you know you are worth it to receive and he will believe you are too!

Start each day by telling yourself something really positive. Do not believe the negative things you think about yourself. You are loved and you are enough. Stop talking down to yourself. Do not compare yourself to others. Comparison will rob you of your self-esteem and self-love. And don't compete with another woman.

Protect your energy and space. Stay away from things and people that drain you with negativity. Practice self-care. Take good care of your body mentally, emotionally and spiritually. You will love yourself more when you fill yourself up, take better care of your needs and don't depend on others.

Practice building up your self-esteem by seeing yourself as an amazing woman who's valuable and worthy of great things in life, including great relationships with men. No matter what happens on the outside, treat yourself with love, care, compassion, kindness and respect inside.

Every day write a list of ten things you love about yourself and the things you are grateful for. Keep looking at that list to remind you of how amazing you truly are. You really are! Write out or print a list of positive affirmations and say them every time a negative thought about yourself comes up. Do not seek out validation from anyone outside of you.

Be happy with who you are and in your own skin. Most importantly, realize you are unique, beautiful, and you are worthy.

Positive affirmations

I am enough
I am worthy
I am a goddess who radiates powerful feminine energy
I know my worth
I am loved
I am love
I love myself
I am beautiful inside and out
I am lovable
I feel safe and secure in my feminine energy
I am free to express myself with my feminine energy
I am divine
I am a goddess

About the Author

Feminine Energy, Self-Love, and Relationship Coach H K Queen is a contemporary force to be reckoned with. Having tapped into the wisdom of what makes male-female relationships work, she guides hundreds of women around the world to seek their divine feminine essence, which she believes is the most powerful resource women have.

H K Queen guides women to move away from struggling in their relationships in order to discover the perfect balance of masculine and feminine energy, which she feels is conducive to the most healing form of love, bonding, and harmony in relationships.

Coach H K Queen believes women have lost track of their innate qualities of truly divine feminine energy. To know one's self-worth is what she teaches her clients. This entails rediscovering your traits of self-love, feminine energy, confidence, receiving, enjoying being in the moment, and sacred pleasure.

She teaches that by seeking no approval from others one begins to discover the unique qualities and beauty that every woman possesses.

Through her teachings, many women have gained insight into what it takes to build a strong foundation for a healthy relationship. When women practice self-care and learn to truly love themselves in their own right, a profound shift takes place in the way men look at her. By allowing men to fully step into their masculine energy, they want to provide and bring great pleasure to a woman who can receive with gratitude.

Every client that H K Queen helps, is a source of inspiration. When she helps women move out of panic, anxiety and trigger mode, a great change occurs. When they do the inner work, a feeling of flow occurs as self-compassion sets in. This will lead to a fun-loving, successful relationship which could lead to a healthy and long-term relationship with a man who cherishes them. Women come to her for her wisdom, optimism and tools she gives which help women become experts at being filled with pleasure which in turn sends out great vibes to the universe. And the universe always delivers!

With great privacy, all sessions are are conducted to help women discover their divine light that they can bring into the world. H K Queen describes the zone of being in your divine femininity as a "feeling of deep peacefulness and It feels beautiful because I am not draining myself by constantly operating in my masculine energy."

Instead, she believes men are born leaders, protectors and providers. Women unfortunately have been thrown off course by thinking they have to do all of those things, which have left men feeling confused and under-appreciated. They no longer know how to proceed with women. Their cause has been shaken by females working from their masculine energy, disarming men from their innate purpose.

Currently, H K Queen is in a beautiful relationship where the polarities are very well balanced.

She wants to help women arrive in this beautiful state of balance and flow and her success rate is nearly 100%. She knew it was her calling to help women from a very early time. She always advised friends who she has loved dearly for many years. She is fiercely loyal to them and protective, just as she is with her clients.

To book a private coaching session with H K Queen or get in touch with her you can visit her website.
http://www.thefeminineboutique.com

Made in United States
Orlando, FL
07 February 2025